Slipknot

Transcribed by Pete Billmann, Jeff Jacobson, and Paul Pappas

ISBN 1-903692-23-7

IMP International Music Publications Limited
Griffin House 161 Hammersmith Road London W6 8BS England

(Sic)

Words and Music by Shawn M. Crahan, Paul Gray, Nathan Jordison and Corey Taylor

Gtrs. 1 & 2: w/ Rhy. Fig. 1, 3 times

Eb5 D5 Eb5 D5 Eb5 D5 Eb5 D5 Eb5 Gb5 F5 D5 Ab5 Eb5 D5 Eb5 D5 Eb5 D5 Eb5 D5 Eb5 Gb5 F5 D5 Ab5

an - y - thing, e - ven if I can't han - dle you! Read - i - ly ei - ther way it bet - ter be. Don't you fuck - in'

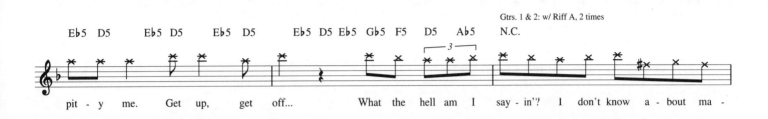

Gtrs. 1 & 2: w/ Riff A, 2 times

Eb5 D5 Eb5 D5 Eb5 D5 Eb5 D5 Eb5 Gb5 F5 D5 Ab5 N.C.

pit - y me. Get up, get off... What the hell am I say - in'? I don't know a - bout ma -

lev - o - lent, sure as hell dec - a - dent. I want some - bod - y to step up, step off.

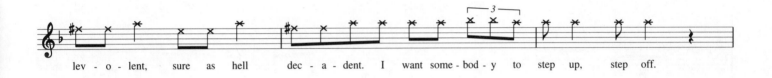

Gtrs. 1 & 2: w/ Rhy. Fig. 1, 1 1/2 times

Eb5 D5 Eb5 D5 Eb5 D5 Eb5 D5 Eb5 Gb5 F5 D5 Ab5 Eb5 D5 Eb5 D5 Eb5 D5 N.C.

Gtrs. 1 & 2 tacet

Walls! Let me fall! Fuck you all! Get a grip, don't let me slip___ till I drop___ the ball!___

Chorus
N.C.

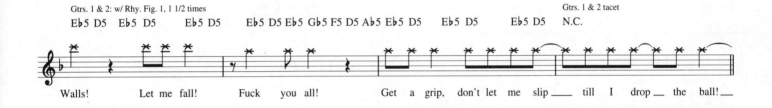

Fuck this shit, I'm sick of it. You're go - in' down, this is a

Gtr. 2 — **Riff B1** — **End Riff B1**

Gtr. 1 — **Riff B** — **End Riff B**

Chorus

Gtrs. 1 & 2: w/ Riffs B & B1

N.C.

Fuck this shit, I'm sick of it. You're go - in' down, this is a

Interlude

N.C.

war! _____

Gtrs. 1 & 2   **Riff C**   **End Riff C**

P.M. _ _ | P.M.   P.M. _ _ | P.M.

Gtrs. 1 & 2: w/ Riff C

Come! _____

Interlude

Eb5   A5   Ab5   Eb5   A5   Gb5   N.C.

play 3 times

(Sing 1st time only)

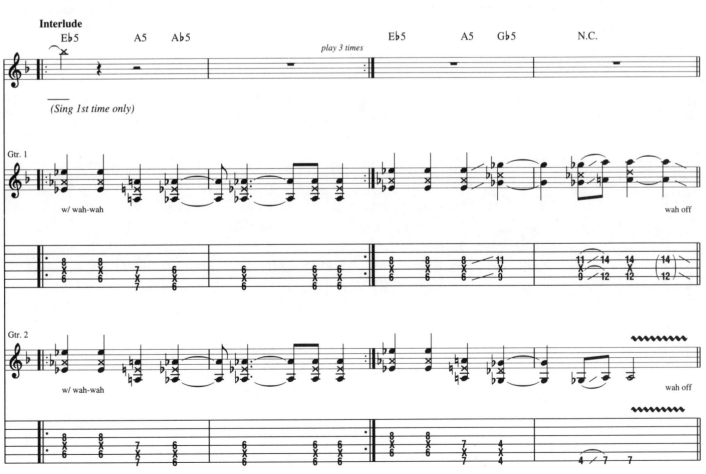

Gtr. 1

w/ wah-wah   wah off

Gtr. 2

w/ wah-wah   wah off

7

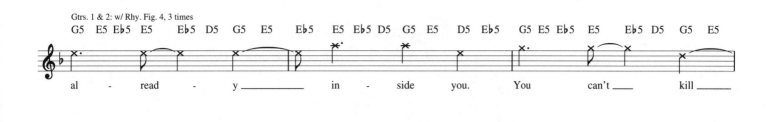

al - read - y _____ in - side you. You can't _____ kill _____

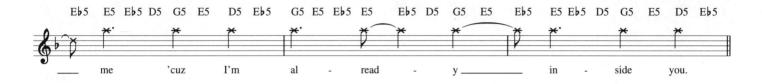

_____ me 'cuz I'm al - read - y _____ in - side you.

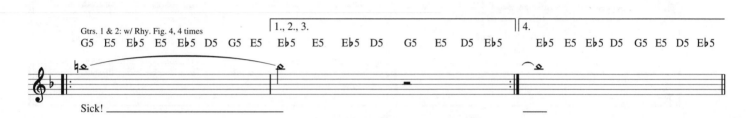

Sick! _____

Yeah! _____

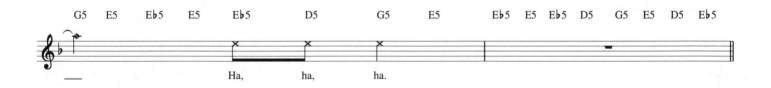

_____ Ha, ha, ha.

Outro
Free Time

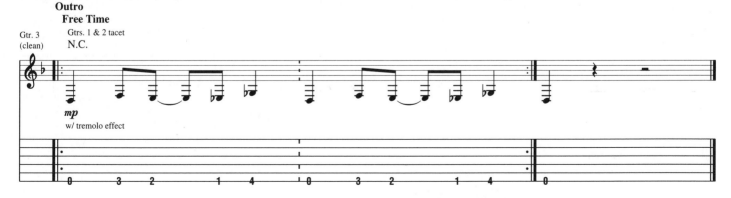

Eyeless

Words and Music by Shawn M. Crahan, Paul Gray, Nathan Jordison and Corey Taylor

* Microphonic fdbk., not caused by string vibration.

** Chord symbols reflect basic harmony.
† composite arrangement

(Sing 1st time only)

Wait and Bleed

Words and Music by Shawn M. Crahan, Paul Gray, Nathan Jordison and Corey Taylor

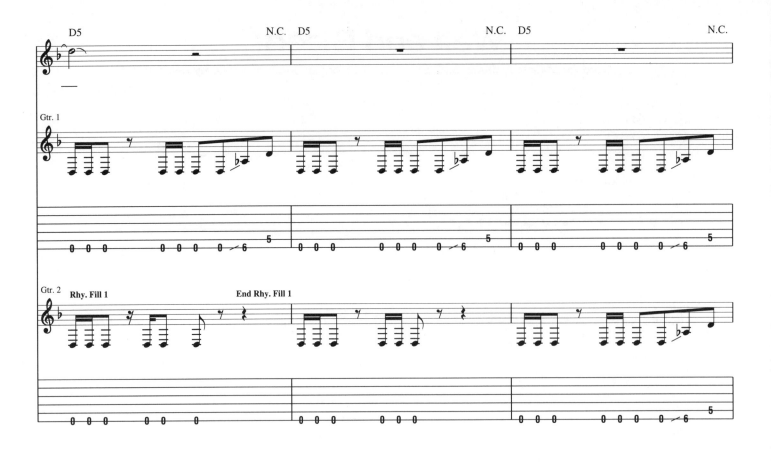

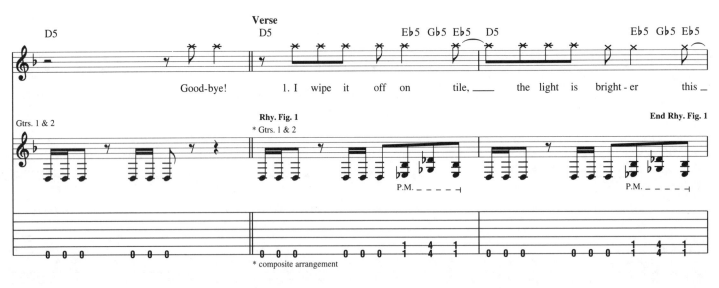

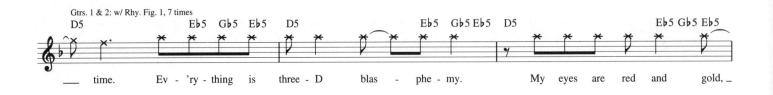

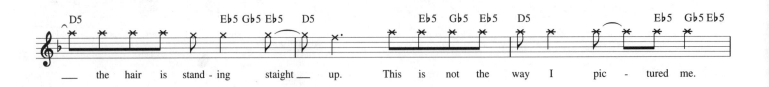

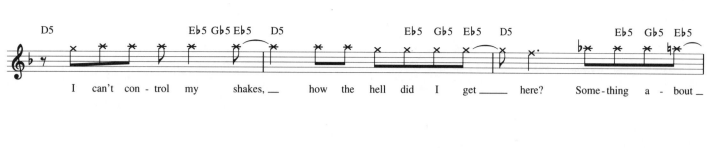

I can't con - trol my shakes, __ how the hell did I get __ here? Some - thing a - bout __

__ this, so ver - y wrong... I have to laugh out loud, __ I wish I did - n't like __

𝄋 Chorus
Gtr. 1: w/ Riff A, 2 times
Gtr. 2: w/ Riff B, 2 times

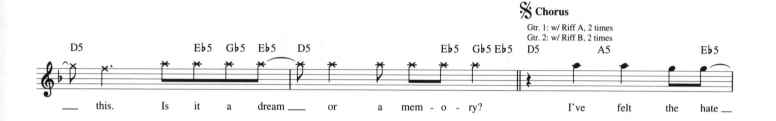

__ this. Is it a dream __ or a mem - o - ry? I've felt the hate __

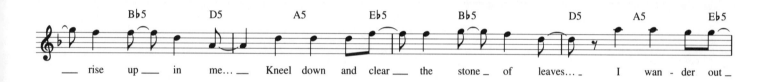

__ rise up __ in me... __ Kneel down and clear __ the stone _ of leaves... _ I wan - der out __

To Coda ⊕

__ where you __ can't see... __ In - side my shell. __ I wait __ and bleed....

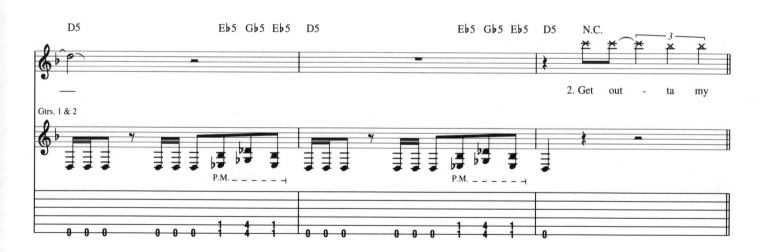

__ 2. Get out - ta my

Gtrs. 1 & 2

P.M. _ _ _ _ _ ┐   P.M. _ _ _ _ _ ┐

Verse
Gtrs. 1 & 2: w/ Rhy. Fig. 1, 4 times

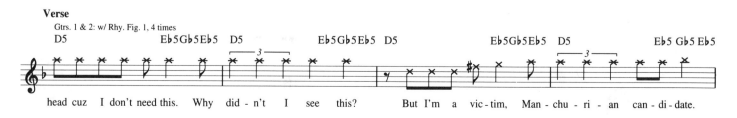

head cuz I don't need this. Why did - n't I see this? But I'm a vic - tim, Man - chu - ri - an can - di - date.

Surfacing

Words and Music by Shawn M. Crahan, Paul Gray, Nathan Jordison and Corey Taylor

Spit It Out

Words and Music by Shawn M. Crahan, Paul Gray, Nathan Jordison and Corey Taylor

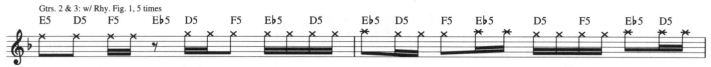

Gtrs. 2 & 3: w/ Rhy. Fig. 1, 5 times

E5 D5 F5 Eb5 D5 F5 Eb5 D5   Eb5 D5 F5 Eb5 D5 F5 Eb5 D5

Big - mouth fuck - er, stu - pid cock - suck - er. Are you scared of me now? Then you're dumb-er then I thought. Al - ways

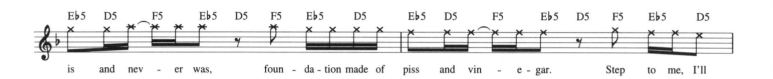

Eb5 D5 F5 Eb5 D5 F5 Eb5 D5   Eb5 D5 F5 Eb5 D5 F5 Eb5 D5

is and nev - er was, foun - da - tion made of piss and vin - e - gar. Step to me, I'll

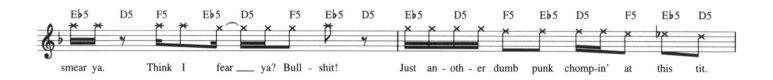

Eb5 D5 F5 Eb5 D5 F5 Eb5 D5   Eb5 D5 F5 Eb5 D5 F5 Eb5 D5

smear ya. Think I fear ___ ya? Bull - shit! Just an - oth - er dumb punk chomp-in' at this tit.

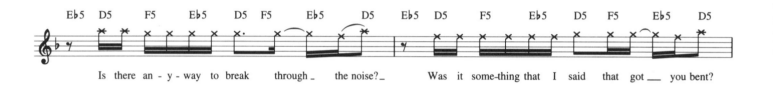

Eb5 D5 F5 Eb5 D5 F5 Eb5 D5   Eb5 D5 F5 Eb5 D5 F5 Eb5 D5

Is there an - y - way to break through ___ the noise? ___ Was it some-thing that I said that got ___ you bent?

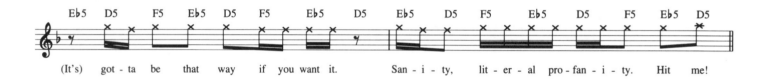

Eb5 D5 F5 Eb5 D5 F5 Eb5 D5   Eb5 D5 F5 Eb5 D5 F5 Eb5 D5

(It's) got - ta be that way if you want it. San - i - ty, lit - er - al pro - fan - i - ty. Hit me!

Chorus

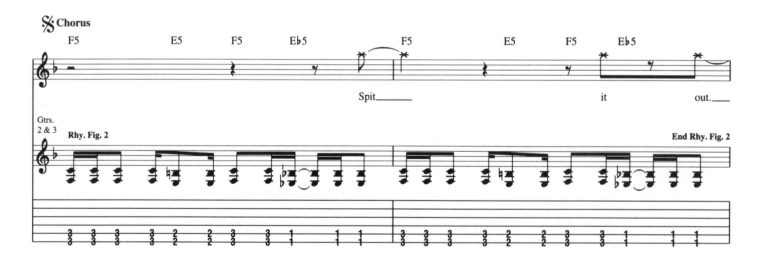

F5 E5 F5 Eb5   F5 E5 F5 Eb5

Spit _____ it out. ___

Gtrs. 2 & 3

Rhy. Fig. 2   End Rhy. Fig. 2

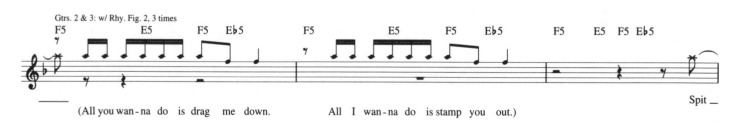

Gtrs. 2 & 3: w/ Rhy. Fig. 2, 3 times

F5 E5 F5 Eb5   F5 E5 F5 Eb5   F5 E5 F5 Eb5

___ (All you wan - na do is drag me down.   All I wan - na do is stamp you out.)   Spit ___

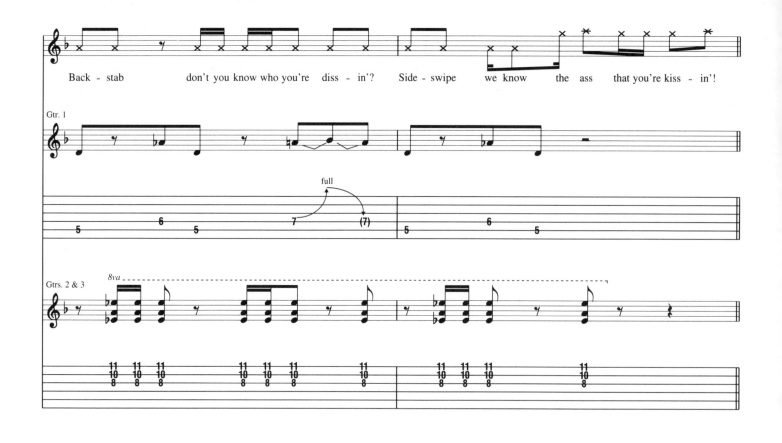

Back - stab   don't you know who you're diss - in'? Side - swipe   we know   the ass   that you're kiss - in'!

Verse

Gtrs. 2 & 3: w/ Rhy. Fig. 1, 4 times

Gtr. 1 tacet

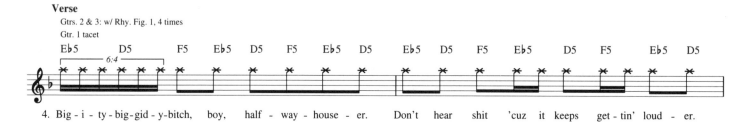

4. Big - i - ty - big-gid - y-bitch, boy,   half - way - house - er.   Don't   hear   shit   'cuz it keeps get-tin' loud - er.

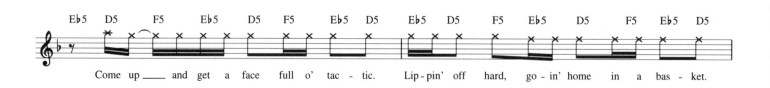

Come up ____ and get a face   full o' tac - tic.   Lip-pin' off hard,   go - in' home   in a   bas - ket.

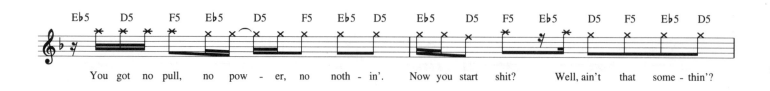

You got no pull,   no pow - er,   no   noth - in'.   Now you start   shit?   Well, ain't   that   some - thin'?

D.S. al Coda

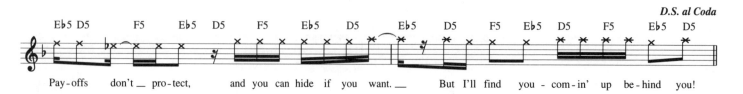

Pay - offs   don't __ pro - tect,   and you can hide if you want. __   But I'll find   you - com - in' up be - hind you!

28

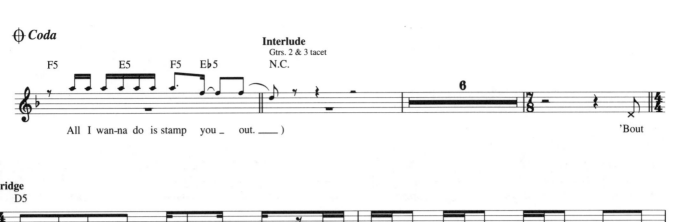

crew and all ___ the fools and all the pol - i - tix. Get your lips read - y, gon - na gag, gon - na make you sick.

You got dick when they passed out the good stuff. Bam - are you sick of me? Good e-nough - had e-nough!

Rhy. Fig. 4

End Rhy. Fig. 4

Tattered and Torn

Words and Music by Shawn M. Crahan, Paul Gray, Nathan Jordison and Corey Taylor

Drop D Tuning; Down 1 1/2 Steps:
① = C#   ④ = B
② = G#   ⑤ = F#
③ = E   ⑥ = B

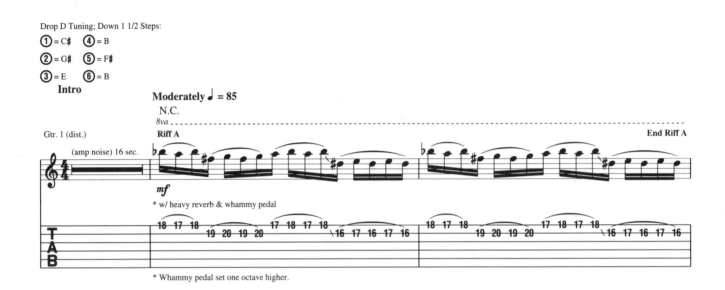

* w/ heavy reverb & whammy pedal

* Whammy pedal set one octave higher.

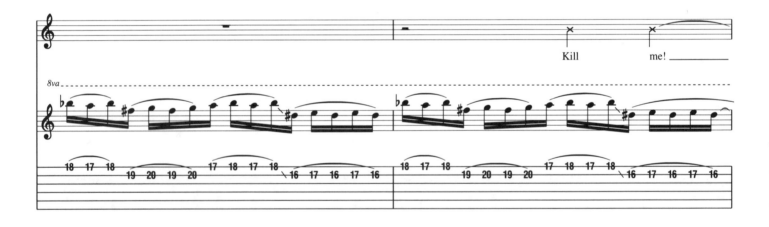

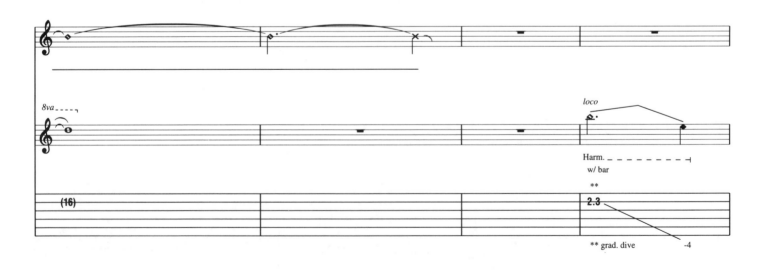

** grad. dive

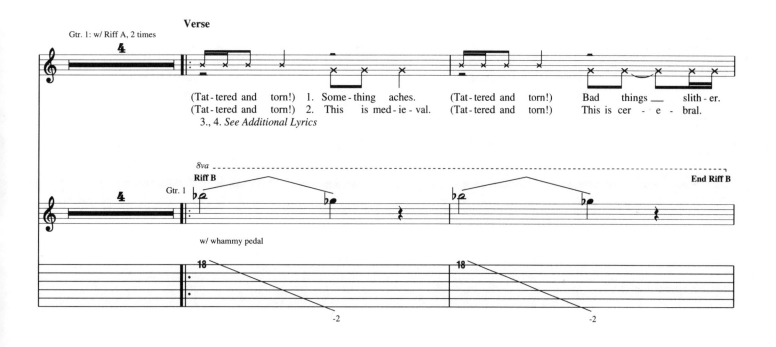

Verse

Gtr. 1: w/ Riff A, 2 times

(Tat-tered and torn!) 1. Some-thing aches. (Tat-tered and torn!) Bad things __ slith-er.
(Tat-tered and torn!) 2. This is med-ie-val. (Tat-tered and torn!) This is cer - e - bral.
3., 4. *See Additional Lyrics*

8va
Riff B
Gtr. 1

w/ whammy pedal

End Riff B

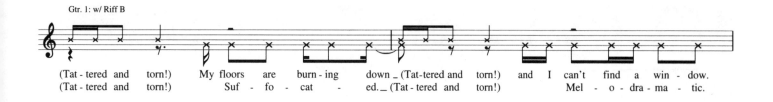

Gtr. 1: w/ Riff B

(Tat - tered and torn!) My floors are burn - ing down __ (Tat-tered and torn!) and I can't find a win - dow.
(Tat - tered and torn!) Suf - fo - cat - ed. __ (Tat-tered and torn!) Mel - o - dra - ma - tic.

1., 2., 3.
Gtr. 1: w/ Riff A, 2 times

4.
Gtr. 1: w/ Riff A, 1 1/2 times

Outro
Gtr. 1 tacet

D5   E♭5 D5   F5 D5   E♭5 D5 F♯5 D5   E♭5 D5   F5 D5   E♭5 D5 F♯5

Rrr! _____   From the things that make __ me hurt!   From the things that make __ me hurt!
(Tear-ing my-self a - part! __   Tear-ing my-self a - part! __

Gtr. 1 *8va*

* Gtr. 2 (dist.)

mf

* doubled throughout

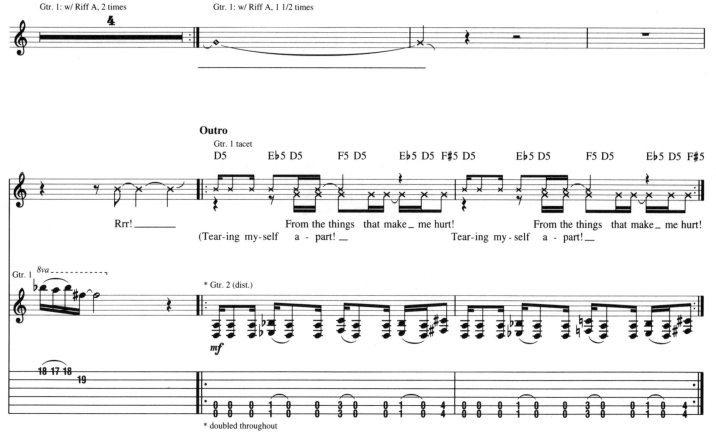

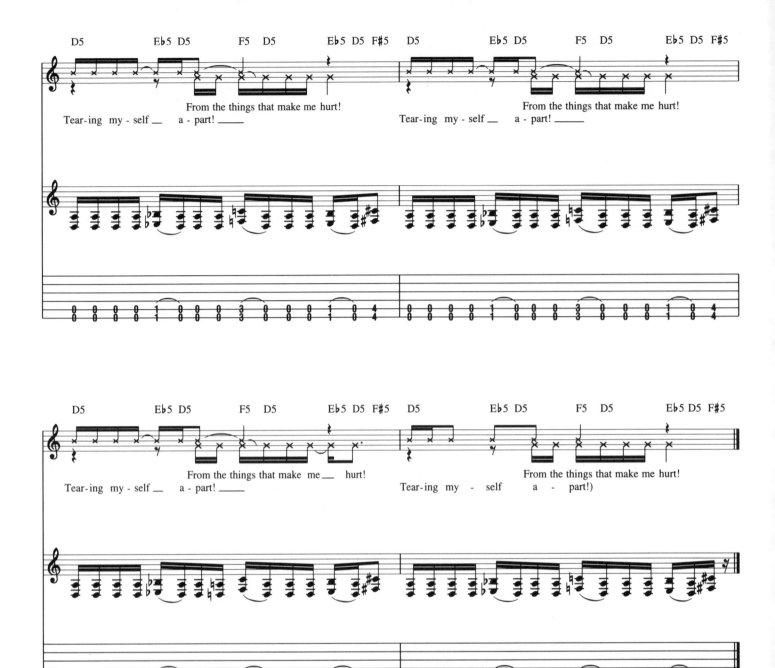

Additional Lyrics

3. (Tattered and torn!) Driven to the verge of...
   (Tattered and torn!) I make you my enemy.
   (Tattered and torn!) The nerves you sever.
   (Tattered and torn!) Can serve you better.

4. (Tattered and torn!) In the blink of an eye.
   (Tattered and torn!) In the spare of a second.
   (Tattered and torn!) Open my wrists.
   (Tattered and torn!) Give me my lessons!

Me Inside

Words and Music by Shawn M. Crahan, Paul Gray, Nathan Jordison and Corey Taylor

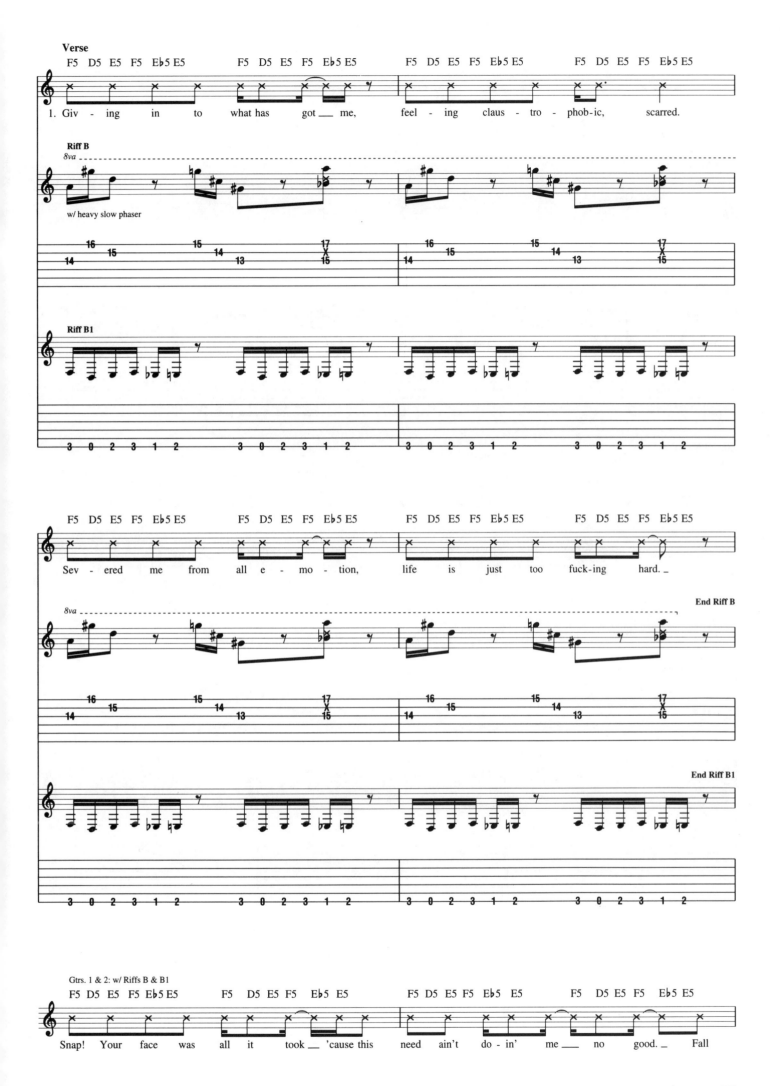

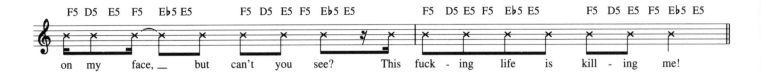

on my face, __ but can't you see? This fuck - ing life is kill - ing me!

Chorus

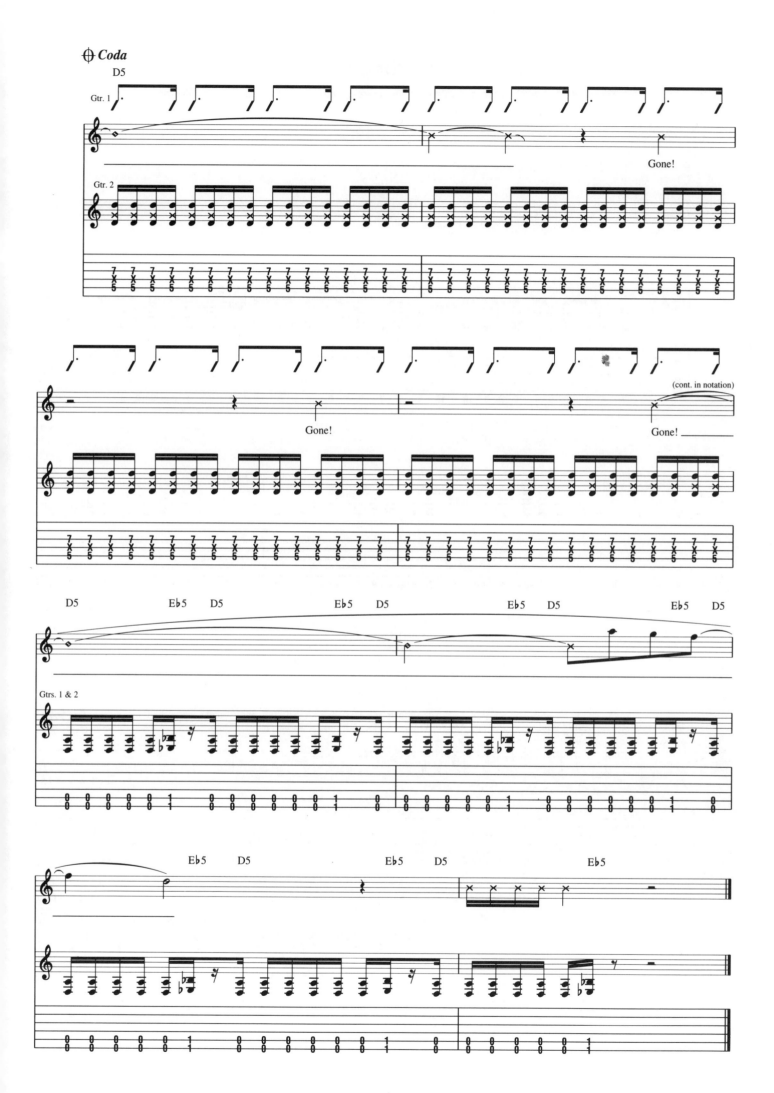

Liberate

Words and Music by Shawn M. Crahan, Paul Gray, Nathan Jordison and Corey Taylor

To Coda ⊕

Eb5 D5

Gtr. 1 tacet
N.C.

(Your gar-bage in is gar-bage out.) Lib - er - ate ___ my mad - ness. ___

Gtrs. 1 & 2

Gtr. 2

P.M.

Chorus
Gtrs. 1 & 2: w/ Rhy. Fig. 1, 4 times

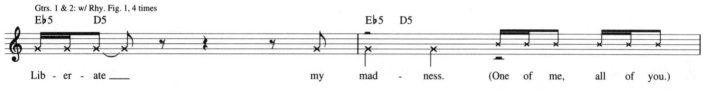

Eb5   D5   Eb5   D5

Lib - er - ate ___ my mad - ness. (One of me, all of you.)

Eb5   D5   Eb5 D5   Eb5   D5

Lib - er - ate ___ my mad - ness. I just want to lib - er - ate ___ my

D.S. al Coda

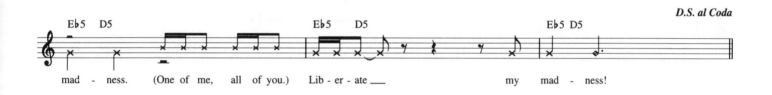

Eb5   D5   Eb5   D5   Eb5 D5

mad - ness. (One of me, all of you.) Lib - er - ate ___ my mad - ness!

⊕ *Coda*

D5 Eb5 D5 Eb5 D5 Eb5   D5 Eb5 D5 Eb5   D5   Eb5 D5 Eb5 D5 Eb5

out.)

Gtrs.
1 & 2 **Rhy. Fig. 3**

End Rhy. Fig. 3

Bridge
Gtrs. 1 & 2: w/ Rhy. Fig. 3, 2 times

D5 Eb5   D5   Eb5   D5   Eb5   D5   Eb5   D5   Eb5   D5

Saved, you're such a slave. I don't ex - pect a name.

You don't care, I was-n't wit-ness. I can't be a part of a sys-tem such __ as this.

Hard eyes glow ___ right in my dark - ness a - gain ___ with the

sick - ness. Ren-e-gade sis-ters, blis-ters, sal-i-vate, lit-i-gate, lib-er-ate, mad-ness,

Gtrs. 1 & 2

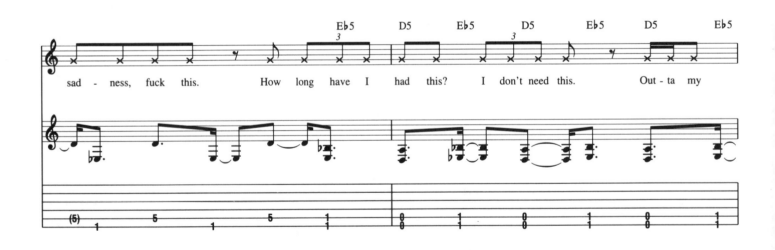

sad - ness, fuck this. How long have I had this? I don't need this. Out-ta my

busi - ness! ___ In - sert, en - gage, be - trayed, my ___ God! ___

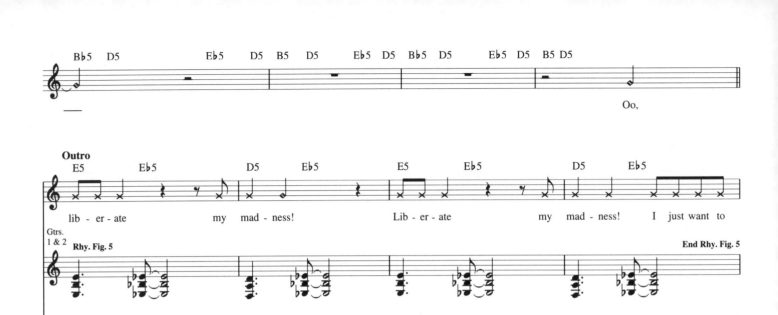

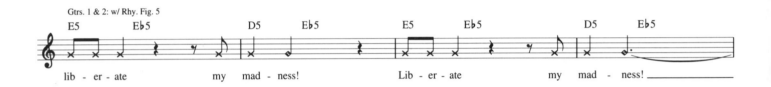

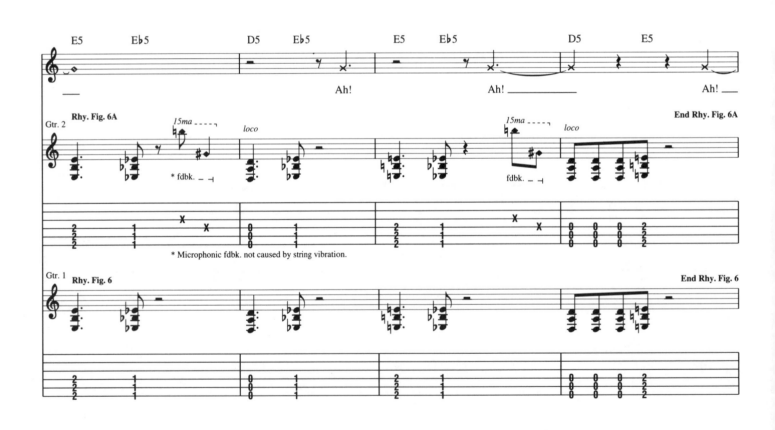

* Microphonic fdbk. not caused by string vibration.

Prosthetics

Words and Music by Shawn M. Crahan, Paul Gray, Nathan Jordison and Corey Taylor

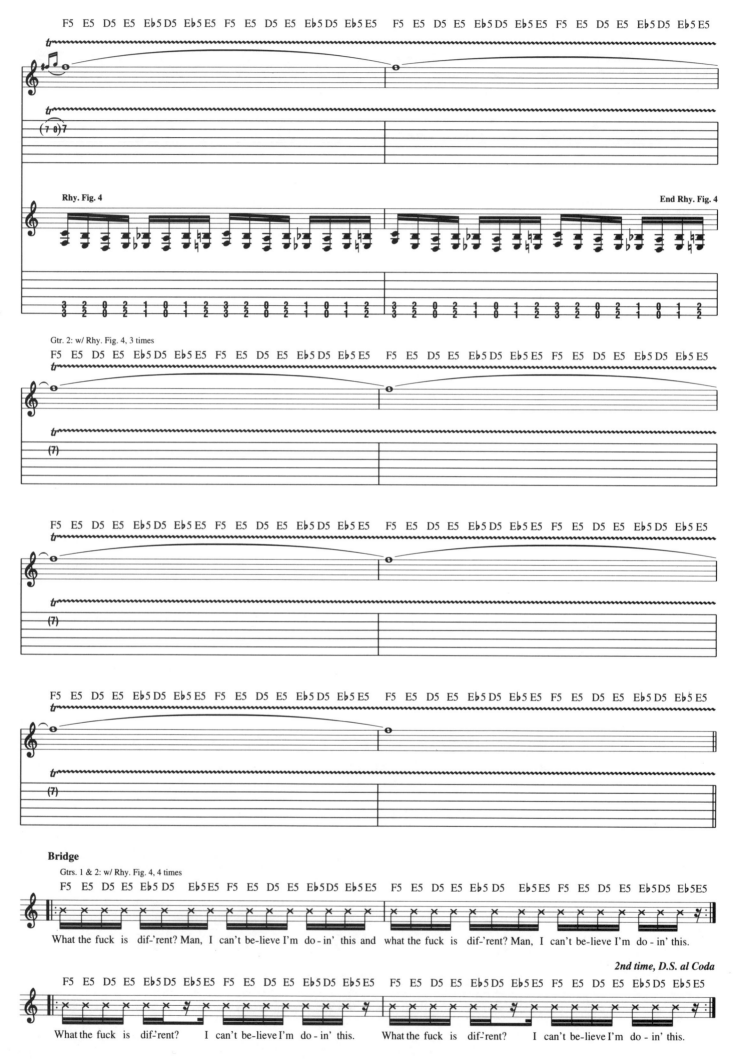

No Life

Words and Music by Shawn M. Crahan, Paul Gray, Nathan Jordison and Corey Taylor

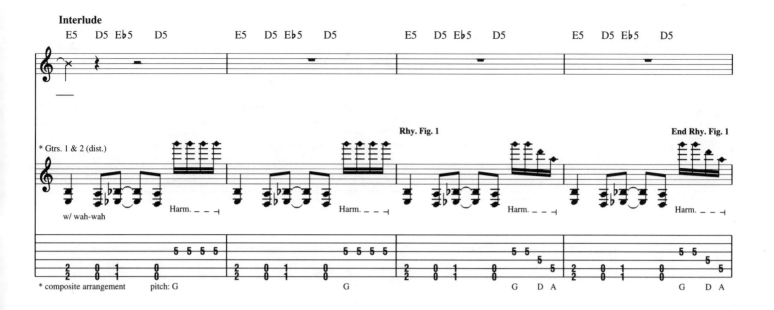

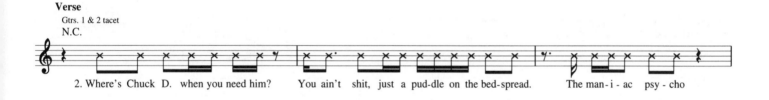

Breathe, A-mer-cult! Breathe! One more seethe! Freak like you got-ta pair.

Won't be my fault __ when you're paint-ed in the cor-ner of a no good life. This is

Chorus
Gtrs. 1 & 2: w/ Rhy. Fig. 2, 2 times, simile

A5   D5   F#5   F5   A5   D5   F#5   F5   A5   D5   F#5   F5   A5   E5   F#5   F5   E5

no kind __ of life! __ This is no kind __ of life! __ It's
(You got to get out!)

To Coda ⊕

A5   D5   F#5   F5   A5   D5   F#5   F5   A5   D5   F#5   F5   A5   E5   F#5   F5   E5

no kind __ of life! __ This is no kind __ of life! __
(You can't blame me!)

Bridge

N.C.   D5   N.C.   D5   N.C.   D5   N.C.   D5

I can't re-mem-ber, I don't un-der-stand. Is it mal-ice that makes you this way?

Gtrs.
1 & 2   **Rhy. Fig. 3**   **End Rhy. Fig. 3**

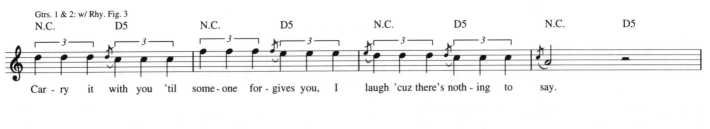

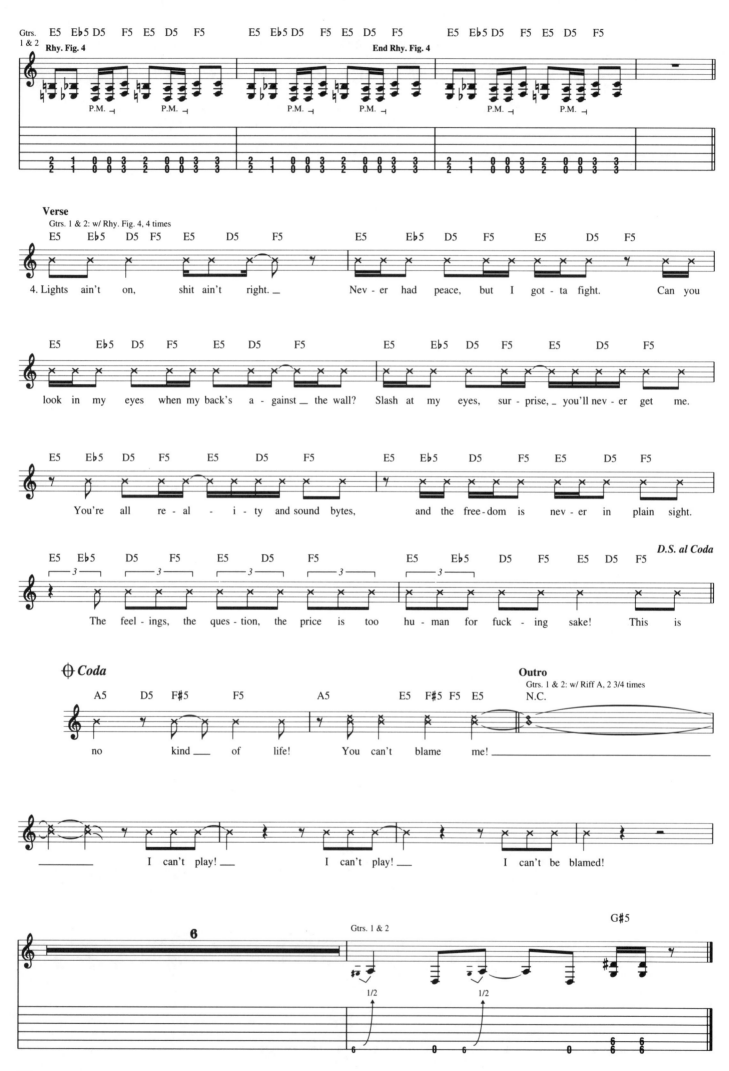

Diluted

Words and Music by Shawn M. Crahan, Paul Gray, Nathan Jordison and Corey Taylor

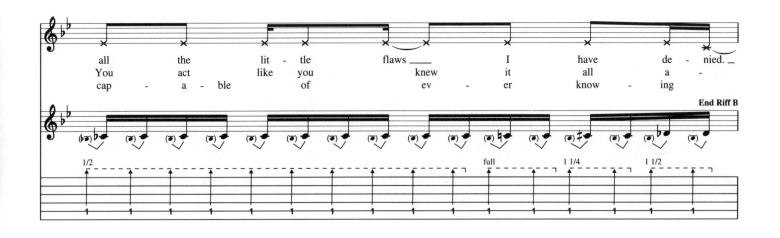

all the lit - tle flaws ___ I have de - nied. ___
You act like you knew it all a -
cap - a - ble of ev - er know - ing

End Riff B

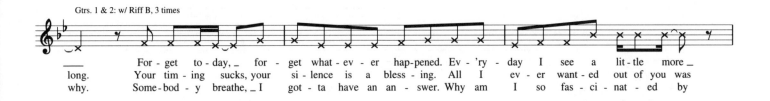

Gtrs. 1 & 2: w/ Riff B, 3 times

___ For - get to - day, _ for - get what - ev - er hap - pened. Ev - 'ry - day I see a lit - tle more _
long. Your tim - ing sucks, your si - lence is a bless - ing. All I ev - er want - ed out of you was
why. Some - bod - y breathe, _ I got - ta have an an - swer. Why am I so fas - ci - nat - ed by

of the world's de - fi - cien - cies. I'm noth - ing short of be - ing one com - plete ca - tas - tro - phe! ___
some - thing you could nev - er be. Now take a real good look at what you've fuck - ing done to me! ___
big - ger pic - tures, bet - ter things? But I don't care what you think; you'll nev - er un - der - stand

Chorus

Fb5   Eb5   Fb5   Eb5   Fb5

___ } me!   What ___ the hell _____ did ___ I ___

Gtrs. 1 & 2   **Rhy. Fig. 2**   **End Rhy. Fig. 2**

Gtrs. 1 & 2: w/ Rhy. Fig. 2, 3 times

Eb5   Fb5   Eb5   Fb5   Eb5   Fb5

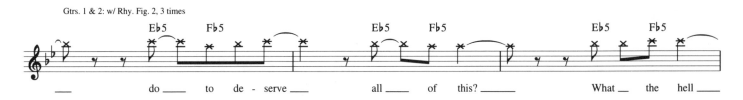

___ do ___ to de - serve ___ all ___ of this? ___ What __ the hell ___

65

Only One

Words and Music by Shawn M. Crahan, Paul Gray, Nathan Jordison and Corey Taylor

Scissors

Words and Music by Shawn M. Crahan, Paul Gray, Nathan Jordison and Corey Taylor

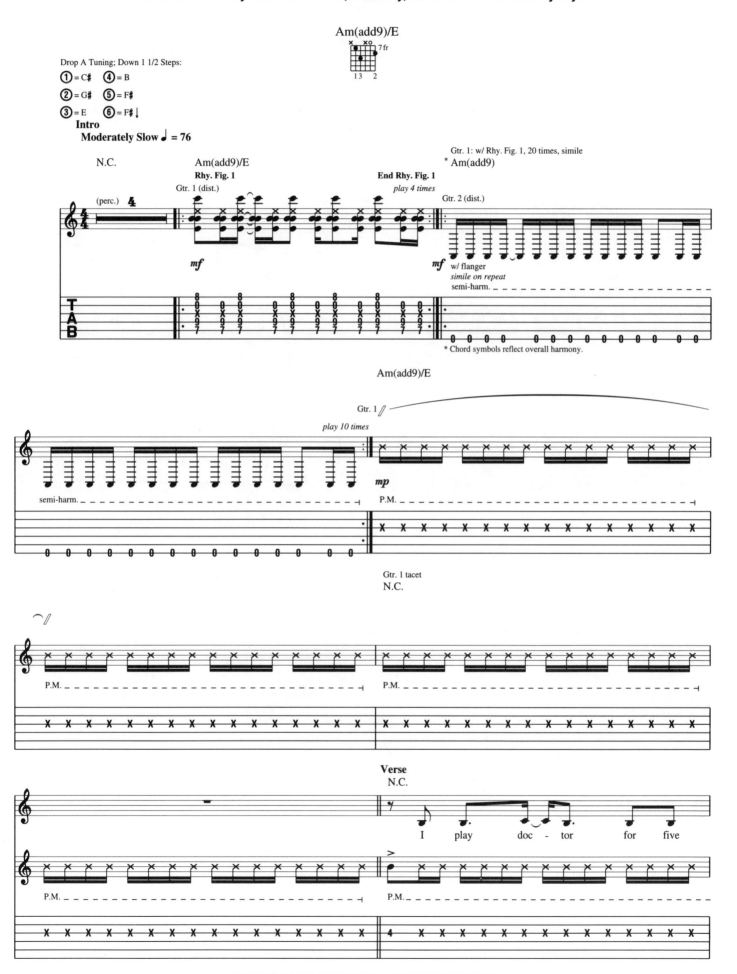

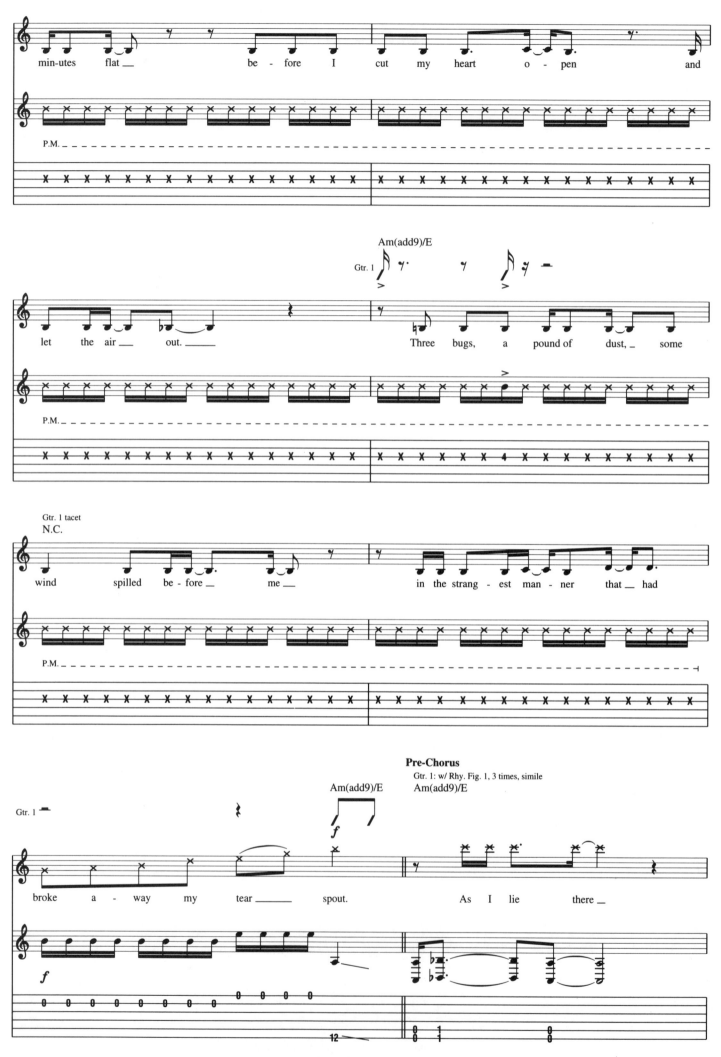

with my tongue spread _ wide o - pen, a black wid - ow had of - fered me _

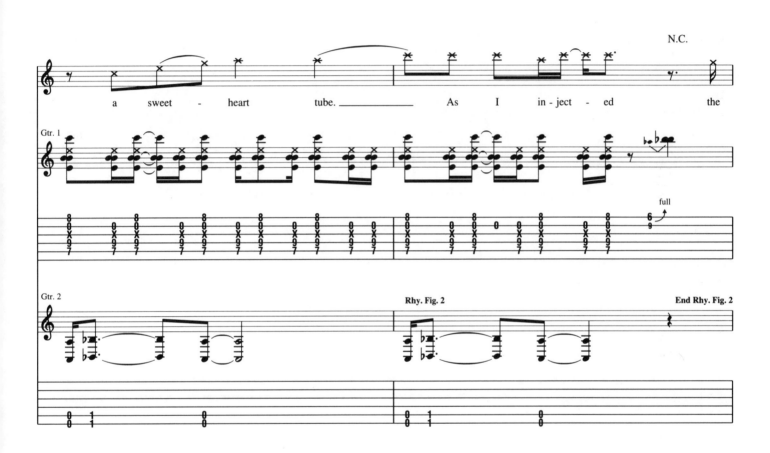

a sweet - heart tube. _____ As I in - ject - ed the

can - died heart that I ____ se - lect - ed, she said, "Don't hes - i - tate, just

do what you have _ to do _ to me!"

Chorus
Gtrs. 1 & 2: w/ Rhy. Fig. 3, 4 times

It's hard to stay be-tween _ the lines of skin. Just 'cause I have nerves, don't mean that I can feel.

I was-n't ver-y much fun to be with an-y-way. Just let the blood run red 'cause I can't feel!

Interlude
Gtr. 1: w/ Rhy. Fig. 1, 4 times, simile
Am(add9)/E

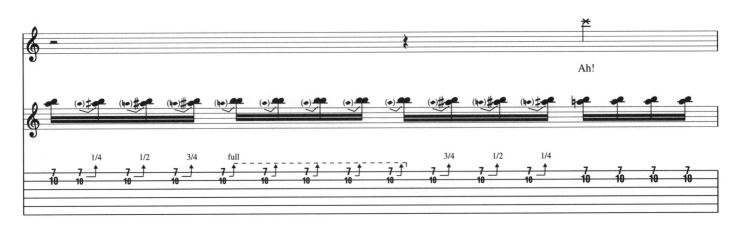

Ah!

Ah!

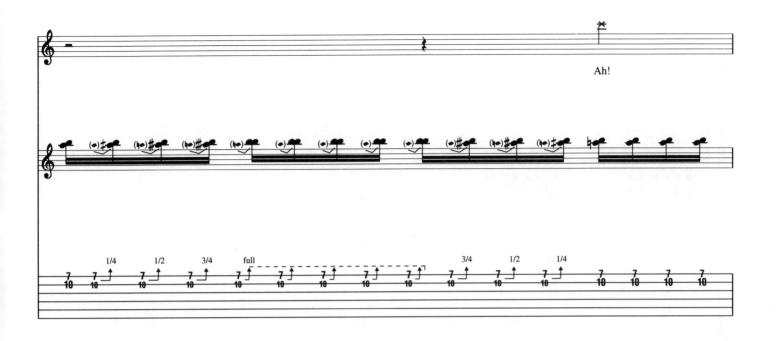

Ah!

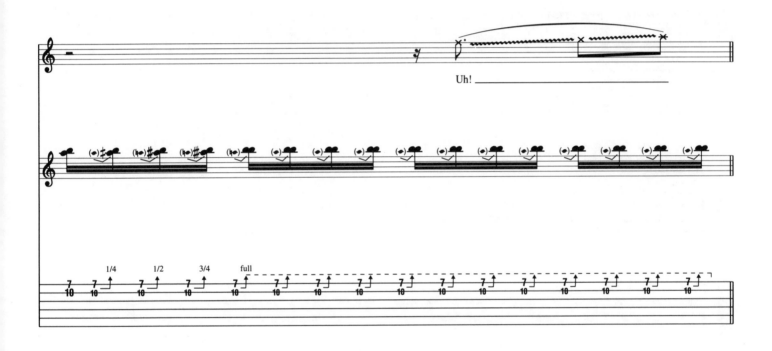

Uh! _____

Chorus

Gtrs. 1 & 2: w/ Rhy. Fig. 3, 4 times

A5 Db5 C5 Bb5 Db5 C5 Bb5 D5   A5 D5   A5 Bb5   A5 Db5 C5 Bb5 Db5 C5 Bb5 D5   A5   D5   A5 Bb5

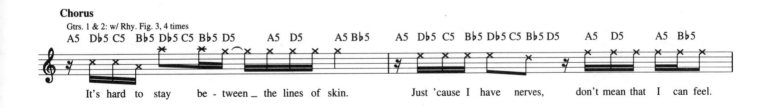

It's hard to stay be - tween _ the lines of skin.   Just 'cause I have nerves,   don't mean that I can feel.

A5 Db5 C5 Bb5 Db5 C5 Bb5 D5   A5 D5   A5 Bb5   A5 Db5 C5 Bb5 Db5 C5 Bb5 D5   A5   D5   A5 Bb5

I was - n't ver - y   much   fun to be with an - y - way.   Just let the blood   run red   'cause I can't   feel!

Gtr. 2: w/ Riff A, 4 times, simile

You are the on-ly one __ that I would rath-er see __ be-fore me.

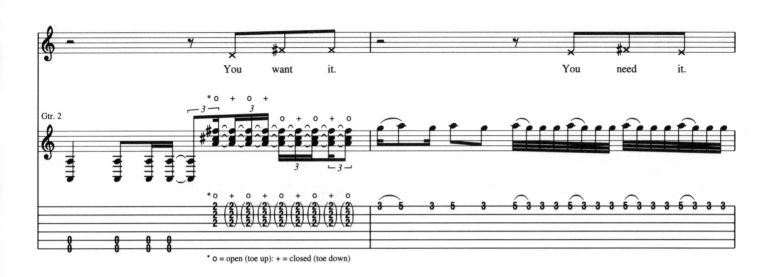

You want it. You need it.

* o = open (toe up): + = closed (toe down)

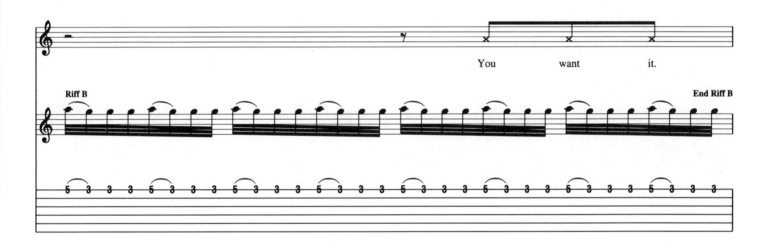

You want it.

Riff B
End Riff B

Gtr. 2: w/ Riff B, 6 times, simile

You need it. You want it. You need it. You want it.

Freely
* Gtr. 1 cont., ad lib., simile
Gtr. 2 tacet

You need it. All right. I die. I die. I die. I die.

* Gtr. 1 continues to play open 5th & 6th strings ad lib., next 14 meas.

I don't want you to be an-y-one when I die. I wan-na die. I'd rath-er

die.   I wan - na die.   You burn.   You burn.   You

burn.   I don't need you an - y - more. _____   I don't need you.

Gtr. 1

P.M. _ _ _ _

Free Time

Gtr. 1 tacet
Lead Voc.: w/ heavy breathing
w/ synth. & percussion

N.C.
(approx. 25 sec.)

A Tempo

N.C.

Ow! _____   It's time. _   It's time. _   It's time. _   It's time. _

A5

It's time. _   It's time. _____   It's time. _   It's time. _

Gtr. 2

Gtrs. 1 & 2

w/o slide
wah-wah off

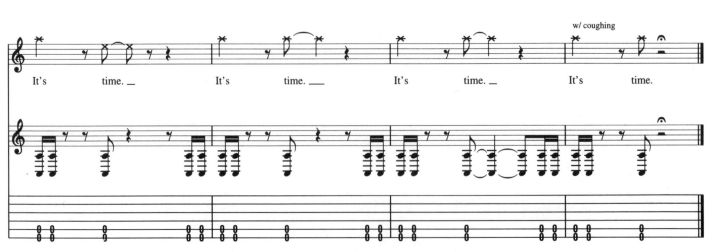

It's time. _   It's time. ___   It's time. _   It's time.

w/ coughing

Eeyore

Words and Music by Shawn M. Crahan, Paul Gray, Nathan Jordison and Corey Taylor

Guitar Notation Legend

Guitar Music can be notated three different ways: on a *musical staff*, in *tablature*, and in *rhythm slashes*.

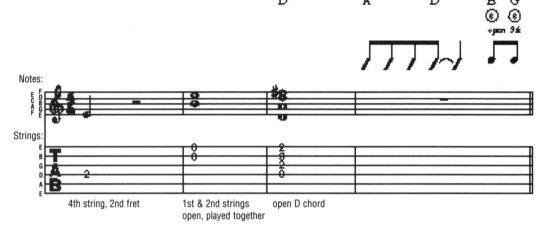

RHYTHM SLASHES are written above the staff. Strum chords in the rhythm indicated. Use the chord diagrams found at the top of the first page of the transcription for the appropriate chord voicings. Round noteheads indicate single notes.

THE MUSICAL STAFF shows pitches and rhythms and is divided by bar lines into measures. Pitches are named after the first seven letters of the alphabet.

TABLATURE graphically represents the guitar fingerboard. Each horizontal line represents a a string, and each number represents a fret.

Notes:

Strings:

4th string, 2nd fret

1st & 2nd strings open, played together

open D chord

Definitions for Special Guitar Notation

HALF-STEP BEND: Strike the note and bend up 1/2 step.

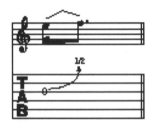

WHOLE-STEP BEND: Strike the note and bend up one step.

GRACE NOTE BEND: Strike the note and bend up as indicated. The first note does not take up any time.

SLIGHT (MICROTONE) BEND: Strike the note and bend up 1/4 step.

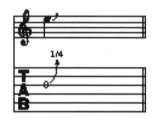

BEND AND RELEASE: Strike the note and bend up as indicated, then release back to the original note. Only the first note is struck.

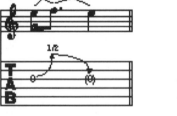

PRE-BEND: Bend the note as indicated, then strike it.

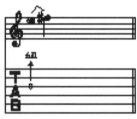

PRE-BEND AND RELEASE: Bend the note as indicated. Strike it and release the bend back to the original note.

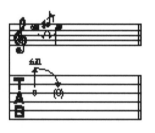

UNISON BEND: Strike the two notes simultaneously and bend the lower note up to the pitch of the higher.

VIBRATO: The string is vibrated by rapidly bending and releasing the note with the fretting hand.

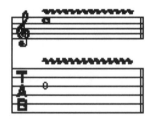

WIDE VIBRATO: The pitch is varied to a greater degree by vibrating with the fretting hand.

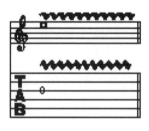

HAMMER-ON: Strike the first (lower) note with one finger, then sound the higher note (on the same string) with another finger by fretting it without picking.

PULL-OFF: Place both fingers on the notes to be sounded. Strike the first note and without picking, pull the finger off to sound the second (lower) note.

LEGATO SLIDE: Strike the first note and then slide the same fret-hand finger up or down to the second note. The second note is not struck.

SHIFT SLIDE: Same as legato slide, except the second note is struck.

TRILL: Very rapidly alternate between the notes indicated by continuously hammering on and pulling off.

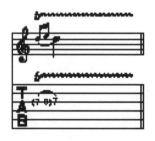

TAPPING: Hammer ("tap") the fret indicated with the pick-hand index or middle finger and pull off to the note fretted by the fret hand.

NATURAL HARMONIC: Strike the note while the fret-hand lightly touches the string directly over the fret indicated.

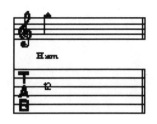

PINCH HARMONIC: The note is fretted normally and a harmonic is produced by adding the edge of the thumb or the tip of the index finger of the pick hand to the normal pick attack.

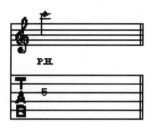

HARP HARMONIC: The note is fretted normally and a harmonic is produced by gently resting the pick hand's index finger directly above the indicated fret (in parentheses) while the pick hand's thumb or pick assists by plucking the appropriate string.

PICK SCRAPE: The edge of the pick is rubbed down (or up) the string, producing a scratchy sound.

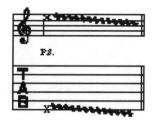

MUFFLED STRINGS: A percussive sound is produced by laying the fret hand across the string(s) without depressing, and striking them with the pick hand.

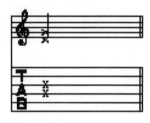

PALM MUTING: The note is partially muted by the pick hand lightly touching the string(s) just before the bridge.

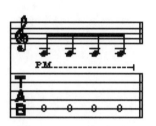

RAKE: Drag the pick across the strings indicated with a single motion.

TREMOLO PICKING: The note is picked as rapidly and continuously as possible.

ARPEGGIATE: Play the notes of the chord indicated by quickly rolling them from bottom to top.

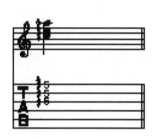

VIBRATO BAR DIVE AND RETURN: The pitch of the note or chord is dropped a specified number of steps (in rhythm) then returned to the original pitch.

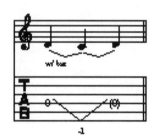

VIBRATO BAR SCOOP: Depress the bar just before striking the note, then quickly release the bar.

VIBRATO BAR DIP: Strike the note and then immediately drop a specified number of steps, then release back to the original pitch.

Additional Musical Definitions

 (accent) • Accentuate note (play it louder)

 (accent) • Accentuate note with great intensity

 (staccato) • Play the note short

 • Downstroke

V • Upstroke

D.S. al Coda • Go back to the sign (𝄋), then play until the measure marked "***To Coda***," then skip to the section labelled "***Coda***."

D.S. al Fine • Go back to the beginning of the song and play until the measure marked "***Fine***" (end).

Rhy. Fig. • Label used to recall a recurring accompaniment pattern (usually chordal).

Riff • Label used to recall composed, melodic lines (usually single notes) which recur.

Fill • Label used to identify a brief melodic figure which is to be inserted into the arrangement.

Rhy. Fill • A chordal version of a Fill.

tacet • Instrument is silent (drops out).

 • Repeat measures between signs.

⌐1. ⌐2. • When a repeated section has different endings, play the first ending only the first time and the second ending only the second time.

NOTE: Tablature numbers in parentheses mean:
1. The note is being sustained over a system (note in standard notation is tied), or
2. The note is sustained, but a new articulation (such as a hammer-on, pull-off, slide or vibrato begins, or
3. The note is a barely audible "ghost" note (note in standard notation is also in parentheses).